Contents

KU-675-987

WITHDRAWN FROM STOCK

Any words appearing in the main text in bold, **like this**, are explained in the Glossary.

A forest in Canada

Imagine walking along a forest path in south-east Canada. It is a fresh spring morning and the last scraps of winter snow lie in the shadows.

Beech, sugar-maple, birch, ash and oak trees are growing new leaves. These are **deciduous** trees – trees that lose their leaves in autumn. There are **evergreen** trees too, such as hemlock, white cedar, red pine and jack pine. These trees have needle-shaped leaves, which they keep for the whole year.

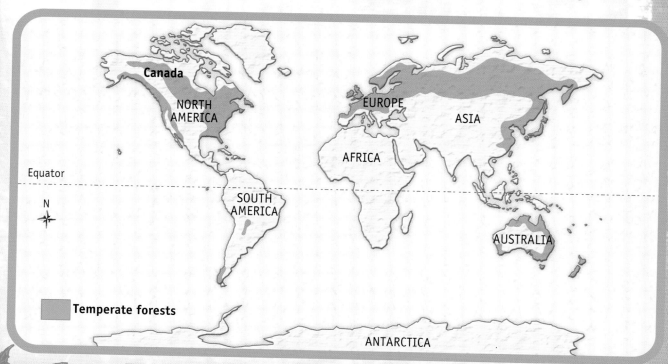

Canada

NORTH AMERICA

EUROPE

ASIA

AFRICA

Equator

N

SOUTH AMERICA

AUSTRALIA

Temperate forests

ANTARCTICA

This map shows the world's temperate forests. Temperate forests grow in areas that have warm summers and cold winters.

A wide variety of plants lives in temperate forests.

Temperate forest

There are several different types of forests. This forest is called a **temperate forest** because it grows in the temperate zone – the part of the world where there are four distinct seasons. The winters are very cold and the summers can be hot. Within this forest there are many **habitats** – places where animals and plants live. You are about to discover the animals and plants that live in these forest habitats.

Explorer's notes

Forest habitats:
- on the leaves
- under the ground
- in the **canopy**
- in the leaf litter
- under bark
- among the grasses.

Forest layers

From the ground, it is easy to see that the forest is made up of different layers. The tallest trees form the **canopy**. This layer of leaves and branches shades the ground. The **understorey** has young trees that may one day become part of the canopy, and short trees that grow best in the shade. The shrub layer is only a metre or so tall. Below this are grasses and wildflowers of the herb layer. A layer of rotting leaves and dead wood covers the forest floor.

canopy

understorey

shrub layer

herb layer

forest floor

A forest consists of various layers, from the forest floor to the canopy.

Animals of the forest layers

Some animals, such as the red fox, live on the forest floor. Birds such as winter wrens stay close to the shrub layer for food and protection. Red-tailed hawks are usually seen soaring above the canopy. Whichever layer these forest animals live in, they have features that help them to survive. These features are called **adaptations**. For example, pine martens have sharp claws to help them climb up tree trunks to feed on bird eggs and **nestlings**.

Ferns grow in the dim light beneath the canopy.

The forest floor

The path has led you deep into the forest. Under the evergreen trees there are dark shadows. Under the **deciduous** trees, the light is uneven. By the time summer comes, the leaves of these trees will have grown and the whole forest floor will be quite dark. Plants need light to grow so few bushes and little grass are found here.

Spotted salamanders

On wet spring nights, spotted salamanders come out from their hiding places among the leaf litter and under the ground. They walk to puddles and creeks to lay their eggs.

Pine needles and fungi

A mat of pine needles lies under a pine tree. Toadstools grow among them. These **fungi** feed on the needles, and break them down into soil.

These toadstools feed on pine needles on the forest floor.

Herbs and grasses

Out in the open, where there is light, vetch, fireweed and violets are sprouting. These ground plants have lain **dormant** (inactive) under the winter snow. Now, the plants need to grow and produce seeds before the next winter.

Herbs and grasses grow in light, open areas of the forest.

Explorer's notes

Description of pine needles:

- long
- thin
- stiff
- waxy
- dark green.

9

Forest insects

The warmth of spring has brought out the insects of the forest in huge numbers. Flies, mosquitoes, midges, wasps and beetles whirr and buzz through the air. There are insects under leaves, and on bark. In fact, everywhere you look there seem to be insects.

Life cycle of a forest insect

Adult pine sawflies emerge from the soil and fly into the pine trees to lay their eggs on pine needles. Within a few weeks, the sawfly grubs hatch and feed on pine needles. Before winter, the grubs will climb to the ground, bury themselves and become **pupae**. Over winter, the adult sawfly forms within.

Pine sawfly grubs feed on pine needles.

Important to the forest

Insects are extremely important in the forest. Many beetles are **decomposers**. Decomposers break down dead leaves and wood into soil. Bees and flies are **pollinators**, carrying **pollen** from flower to flower. Perhaps most importantly, insects are food for so many of the forest's other animals, from spiders to birds.

Thousands of beetle species live in the forest.

Explorer's notes

Plants pollinated by insects:
- fireweed
- violet
- vetch
- clover.

A forest glade

The path suddenly opens up at a **glade**, a small clearing in the forest. Grass grows thickly here because the light is bright. A white-tailed deer is grazing. She looks up after every few mouthfuls. She is alert. Then you see why. A fawn just a few hours old is tottering alongside her. This youngster would make an easy meal for a wolf or a lynx.

A white-tailed deer fawn must stay close to its mother for protection.

Snakes

Something is slithering on a rocky outcrop in the centre of the glade. Many garter snakes are there, sunning themselves. They have spent the winter sheltering among those rocks, under the snow. Now they are warming themselves before hunting for frogs and fish in a nearby creek.

Garter snakes need to warm their bodies in the sun to be active.

Porcupines

In winter, porcupines huddle together to keep warm. They find shelter among rocks or fallen timber. In spring, the porcupines each go their own way.

Explorer's notes

Porcupine food:

Winter – pine needles, pine bark.

Spring – maple bark, dandelions, clovers, violets, thorn apples, currants.

End of hibernation

Beneath a fallen tree there is a large hole with branches strewn around it. The soil is flattened by many footprints. You hear a growl and look down into a gully. A black bear is drinking from a creek. There is a cub with her. The bear growls again and leads her cub further into the forest.

Explorer's notes

Description of a black bear:
- shaggy and thick black fur
- long claws
- no tail
- rounded head
- heavy body.

This black bear and her cub are moving through the forest.

Surviving winter

Winter in the forest is very cold and there is not much food available. To survive, the black bear **hibernates**. This means that last autumn she settled down inside her den and fell deeply asleep. A month later, her cub was born. During her hibernation, the bear's heartbeat slowed and her body temperature fell a few degrees. These changes save energy. The bear is able to survive using the fat stored in her body the previous summer.

A black bear and her newborn cub in her winter den.

Woodchuck hibernation

When the woodchuck hibernates, its heartbeat drops from 80 beats a minute to four, and its breathing slows from 28 breaths a minute to one breath a minute.

Bird arrivals

The forest is alive with the calling of birds. Many have recently arrived from the south. They flew there the previous autumn to escape the cold winter. They have returned to build nests and raise their young.

Among these birds are many **species** of wood warblers. Some of these **migratory** birds have flown several thousand kilometres from South America. They arrive in time to feast on the insects and grubs that have appeared.

Many species of wood warblers are migratory birds.

Birds in Europe

In the forests of Europe, birds such as the nightingale and pied flycatcher arrive in spring after spending the winter in Africa.

Good and bad years

If spring is very warm, there may be many insects. Insects can survive best in warm weather, when there is plenty of food available. This means that insect-eating birds will have plenty to eat and may raise several broods. But if spring is cold, very few insects may appear and so insect-eating birds might not raise any chicks at all. Many birds may have to return south to find food.

A warm spring means there will be plenty of insects to feed to the chicks.

Explorer's notes

Birds arriving in spring:
- yellowthroats
- tree swallows
- cedar waxwings
- black-billed cuckoos
- American redstarts
- yellow-bellied sapsuckers.

17

Tree trunks

A sharp hammering sounds from above. A yellow-bellied sapsucker is hard at work. This bird is a type of woodpecker and it is using its sturdy beak to drill holes in the bark. **Sap** will flow from these holes and attract insects, which feed on it. When they do, the sapsucker is waiting to snap them up with its long tongue, along with a little of the sap.

Explorer's notes

Bark descriptions:

Pine – rough, dark, with deep furrows and sticky sap.

Beech – green-grey, smooth.

Oak – rough, with patches of lichen.

The feet of the yellow-bellied sapsucker are excellent for perching on tree trunks.

Feet adaptations

The yellow-bellied sapsucker's feet have two toes facing forwards and two facing backwards. This enables them to cling to tree trunks. Their tails are very stiff and give the birds excellent support when hammering at a trunk.

Nuthatches and brown creepers also feed on tree trunks. These birds have long claws for gripping the bark as they search for insects and spiders.

A white-breasted nuthatch searches for insects on a tree trunk.

Red and white

Red-breasted nuthatches prefer to look for food on pine trees, but white-breasted nuthatches prefer **deciduous** trees – trees that lose their leaves in autumn.

Seed eaters

A bird lands on a branch of a pine tree. It has a thick, short beak, but the two parts of the beak seem to have been twisted apart, as if the bird has been in an accident. But it hasn't. This bird is the crossbill and its beak is meant to be like that. The crossbill inserts its beak under one of the scales of a pine cone and prises it away to expose the seed beneath. In a day, a crossbill may collect 1000 seeds.

The red crossbill's beak may be unusual, but it is a useful tool.

Explorer's notes

Seed eaters of the forest:
- red crossbills
- grey squirrels
- eastern chipmunks
- meadow voles
- Clark's nutcrackers.

Collecting seeds

Warm days make the pine cones open up and drop their seeds. Chipmunks and squirrels scurry across the forest floor to collect this food. The seeds they do not eat will be stored in their underground chambers for the following winter.

Spreading oaks

Squirrels also bury acorns, the fruit of oak trees, as a winter food supply. Sometimes the squirrels don't return and, in the following spring, the acorns sprout and grow into new oak trees. In this way, squirrels help oaks to spread.

Predators and prey

On a stump at the edge of an open space, a large bird is watching the ground. It is a great grey owl, and it is hunting. The owl is a **predator** with keen sight and hearing. In winter, it can even hear a mouse rustling about beneath a metre of snow.

The great grey owl may sit still on a branch for hours while it waits for prey to appear.

Powerful owl

In the forests of Australia, the powerful owl hunts at night for small mammals such as possums and gliders.

Owls and voles

An important food of owls are voles. These small **mammals** make good **prey** for the owls because they grow very quickly and they can breed before they are three weeks old. If there are many seeds, the numbers of voles can soar. In these times of plenty, owls may raise many chicks. But if vole numbers fall, many owls may starve.

The owl takes off. It flies silently. Its wings have special feathers that muffle sound. The owl drops, talons outstretched, to catch its meal.

Voles come out from their burrows to find food.

Explorer's notes

Large predators of the forest:
- black bears
- wolves
- lynxes
- red foxes
- great grey owls
- broad-winged hawks.

Summer fires

In late summer, when timber and air are dry, and temperatures high, a lightning strike can cause a forest fire. If winds are strong, the fire may even burn the forest **canopy**. For many animals, this is a disaster. Food supplies are destroyed and many animals are caught up in the flames and die. But forest fires are a natural part of the life of a forest.

A summer fire can move very fast through a dry forest.

Explorer's notes

Forest fire conditions:
- dry timber and leaf litter
- dry air
- hot weather
- strong winds
- lightning strikes.

Effects of fire

Forest fires kill many tree seedlings. This opens up the forest for grass and other ground plants to grow. Small **mammals** that feed on these plants, such as mice, can increase sharply in number. This brings **predators**. The great grey owl makes use of burnt stumps as perches to scan the ground for **prey**.

Grasses grow soon after a fire.

Helpful regrowth

In the years after fire, many tree seeds sprout and grow densely. This helps snowshoe hares avoid predators such as lynxes. A lynx finds it very difficult to catch a snowshoe hare dodging and weaving among this regrowth.

Autumn in the forest

When days shorten and nights are cool, summer is coming to an end. The animals and plants of the forest prepare for the cold winter.

Plants

Deciduous trees begin to lose their leaves. If they held their leaves over winter, the leaves would freeze solid, die and fall off. The trees would lose valuable **nutrients**. So, each tree transfers nutrients from the leaves and stores them in its trunk. As this happens, the leaves turn yellow or red, then brown. Then they fall.

Deciduous trees are most colourful in autumn.

Evergreen trees, such as pine trees, keep their leaves. Pine needles have very little **sap** and snow slides off them. Their dark colour absorbs the little heat there is. These **adaptations** keep these leaves from freezing solid.

Animals

The birds that **migrated** from the south in spring now return south. With them are the young they raised over the summer.

Mammals begin to slow down, to save energy. Chipmunks and squirrels top up their stores of nuts and black bears prepare their dens.

Winter camouflage

During autumn, snowshoe hares moult their brown hair and grow a white coat for winter. With its white winter coat, the snowshoe hare is almost invisible against the snow. But when the snow melts, the snowshoe hare moults this winter fur and grows a brown coat.

Forest future

Change is a part of the life of a forest. There are changes that take place over a day, and from season to season. Temperature, light and rainfall are among these changes. There are also the changes that occur only occasionally. Fierce fires and wild storms are examples. Forest animals and plants have lived with these changes and survived them. But some change is so great that they cannot survive.

This forest area has recently been cleared.

Explorer's notes

Why forests are important:
- places to visit
- peacefulness
- **habitats**
- unpolluted
- wild.

Deforestation

About 11 000 years ago, the forests of Canada were destroyed by an ice sheet from the north. In the last 300 years, logging and land-clearing for farms, roads and cities has caused **deforestation**.

Conservation

We know now that without forests many forest animals will disappear. People do not want this to happen. They are taking action. Action includes studying forests and setting them aside as national parks.

Use resources wisely

The more forest products we use, the more forests are cut down. Use paper, wood and even water wisely, not wastefully. This will help save forests.

This scientist is studying how forest plants and animals live.

Visit a forest near you. Observe the different kinds of habitats you see. Observe the animals and plants you see in these places. Observe the forest at different times of the year to find out what changes occur.

Using the Internet

Explore the Internet to find out more about forest habitats. Websites can change, so if the link below no longer works, don't worry. Use a kid-friendly search engine, such as www.yahooligans.com or www.internet4kids.com, and type in keywords such as 'forest animals', or even better, the name of a particular forest animal.

Website

http://archive.greenpeace.org/kidsforforests
The website Kids for Forests is a good site to find out about what's happening to forests around the world. It has interactive and factual information.

Disclaimer
All the Internet addresses (URLs) given in this book were valid at the time of going to press. However, due to the dynamic nature of the Internet, some addresses may have changed or ceased to exist since publication. While the author and publisher regret any inconvenience this may cause readers, no responsibility for any such changes can be accepted by either the author or the publisher.

Glossary

adaptation   feature of an animal or plant that helps it to survive

camouflage   colours and patterns that help an animal to hide in its habitat

canopy   highest layer of leaves in a forest

deciduous   sheds leaves (usually in autumn)

decompose   decay or rot

deforestation   removal of trees or forests

dormant   inactive

evergreen   retains leaves for the whole year

fungus   (plural: fungi) mushrooms or toadstools

glade   open space in a forest

habitat   place where an animal or a plant lives

hibernate   become dormant over winter

mammal   animal that drinks its mother's milk when it is young

migrate   move from one place to another

nestling   young bird still in the nest

nutrient   substance that nourishes living things

pollen   powdery material produced by flowers

pollination   transfer of pollen from flower to flower

predator   animal that kills and eats other animals

prey   animal that is killed and eaten by other animals

pupa   (plural: pupae) stage in the life cycle of many insects, between larva and adult

sap   thick liquid that flows through a plant

species   group of living things that reproduce with each other

talon   claw of a raptor (bird of prey)

temperate forest   forest of the temperate zone

understorey   layer of plants that grows beneath the tallest trees in a forest

Index